The Presence

To Rob Steiner —
whose name has been a genuine
and welcome presence in the class —

Keep the faith —

[signature]

01/12/99.

The Presence

Bruce Meyer

BLACK MOSS PRESS

1999

Published by Black Moss Press, 2450 Byng Road, Windsor, Ontario N8W 3E8. Black Moss Press books are distributed by Firefly Books, 3680 Victoria Park Ave., Willowdale, Ontario, M2H 3K1. All orders should be directed there.

Black Moss Press would like to acknowledge the support of the Department of Canadian Heritage.

We would also like to acknowledge the support of the Canada Council for the Arts for our publishing program.

Canadian Cataloguing in Publication Data

Meyer, Bruce, 1957-
     The presence

Poems.
ISBN 0-88753-319-1

     I. Title.

PS8576.E93P74 1998   C811'.54   C98-901050-3
PR9199.3.M49P74 1998

Acknowledgments

Some of these poems have appeared previously in *The Cumberland Review, Descant, Eclectic Literary Forum, Edge City Review, Exile, The Fiddlehead, The Hamilton Spectator, The Hart House Review, Light* and *The Ottawa Citizen*. Several poems were selected by Robert Sward for inclusion in *Pares cum Paribus* (Chile) and translated into Spanish by Oscar Aguilera.

"Chinatown" won the 1998 Ruth Cable Memorial Prize for Poetry. The author is grateful to the editors, Cynthia Erbes and Suzanne Neubauer of *Eclectic Literary Forum* for their support and enthusiasm.

The cover art was supplied through the good advice and gracious efforts of Guenter Dreeke of the Dickinson Gallery, Toronto. The front cover art is a British steel engraving by Charles Knight, c. 1860, of a statue by Carlo Finelli (1786-1853) titled "Love Reviving Life." The statue is currently part of the collection at Chatsworth House, Derbyshire, England.

The author is grateful to the following individuals for their advice, support, encouragement and suggestions: Dana Gioia, David Mason, Molly Peacock, Alfred Corn, Sydney Lea, Robert Sward, Ray Robertson, Kim Echlin, Mary Barrie, Michael Peich, Elise Gervais, Carolyn Meyer, G. Homer Meyer, Margaret Meyer and Kerry Johnston. Special thanks to Marty Gervais and the staff of Black Moss Press.

This book is for Kerry and Katie

They believed that the world was made of things they could not touch nor see, as they knew that behind the basket their hands made was the shape of the perfect basket which once made would endure for ever beyond the time when its semblance was broken and worn thin by use. So they knew that the shape of to-morrow lingered just beyond to-day, and that to-day the people made to-morrow's basket. Each man hoped to see what his hands were doing, and no man could. Each man sought the shadow beyond the work, and no man could reach it.

—*Howard O'Hagan,* Tay John

The Melting

—for David Mason

Be still. Breathless. On your hat
rests the individualization of art
in nature, the innocent upstart
of divinity made mortal by all that
fails in us to see. Dead cold begat
perfection, the cold that shuns life,
the icy, heavenly indifference rife
with sad desire.

                    We know He sat
upon the stars and made the Earth,
rhymed it with whales, squirrels; know
He loved resonances, the small mirth
of making and remaking life to sow
constancy in change and death in rebirth.
God's sonnet is the melting snow.

Cottage

It was the rain falling in imitation of silence,
a softness in the air coaxing the perfume of pine
from sentinels beyond the screen-covered porch
and the hiss of white stocking in the naphtha lamp
that signaled the darkness of our still presence.
Air rising from your lips, almost a word, the damp
unformed syllables that will not sound, is a line
waiting to be written, a poem of your touch.

This is a large land, my dreams tell me, a place
where I wake in the deadened night, so cold a toe
dare not move beneath sheets, a realm not stone
but imagination, afterthought, a memory to retreat
to in the name of isolation. A moth tries to trace
the outline of frame, battering against the sweet
temptation of the only daylight still aglow,
and finding that star constant and impossible, alone

and wearied, falls into the darkness and complains
no more. I rise, not wishing to wake you. The song
of old seasons hidden in the wicker web betrays me.
Crossing the demi-threshold to the lounge, the air
is suddenly strange, smelling of old books and long-
lost summers of imaginings, the sad sweetness of free
ash souring in the grate, and above it the tiny grains
of schist in the hearthstone shine like the many stars

that lie hidden by the aftermath of failed expectations.
In the kitchen, where I open a beer, setting aside enough
counter amid the supper dishes we have left for mice,
I remember the comings and goings of friends, the slow
mornings when the steam from coffee cups rose in rough
curls that moved faster than us. Where are the anticipations?
There is no time here, although eternity would be nice.
But tomorrow we return, and the dream is over now.

Big Things Dancing

Driving the Transcanada is endless;
driving it at night insane. We head
along the road, fight the need to nap
and measure the miles to our next stop.

The sharp eye is deluded by darkness,
lulled by the drift of rain and road,
and ushered further by eerie shape.
If we hit a moose there is no escape.

Mile after mile we say nothing, confess
nothing and hide our fears. Ahead,
there is only the destination our map
points us to, mere chance and trap.

A yellow diamond glares a charging moose,
a sign of big things dancing like dead
hopes suddenly alive and well. Snap
out of it now. We are nowhere on the map.

My Computer Sleeping: A Lullaby

Hush-a-bye you diode pile.
Save your screen, make Daddy smile.
Leave the busy world to fret,
dream of sites on the Internet.

Dream of servers and cd rom,
a place for you in every home
'til darkness passes and you are freed
by soft commandings gently keyed.

Guardian angels stand by you
that surge protectors may be true.
Let all your circuits wake up bright
guided by watts and mega bite.

Pray your user is your friend,
that every warranty may extend
another year before you meet
a future that makes you obsolete.

Mississippi Rain

—for Angela Ball and Kim Herzinger

Let's go travelling in my memory...
the first hyacinths blooming
in the iron-scented slurry
of dripping eaves flowing

into resurrected shoots,
the air almost liquid as sky,
catches a spark of ash and ignites
across the widow-veiled mystery

of a southern night. One could
almost believe that in this place
legends live eternally, the blood
lines drawn up like old rivers pace

to find a delta, an open mouth
to shout out their pity and despair,
all in the name of the place south
of whatever is somewhere

in the geography of the senses.
We make our own stories, those
of us who simply visit such places,
listen, learn and wonder, choose

our own beginnings, dignify our
own ends, and let the rest be song.
Lightning flashes its sudden power,
illumining, but not for long.

The steady measure of the storm
has passed away like music heard
from a distant house; light, warm
and inviting in the window, a bird

lamenting a sad, unnameable tune.
We flick our cigarettes like comets
falling through the black and soon
the world is made of thoughts

and each dream is another journey.
Think about it now. Mind and heart
lead us through an amazing memory,
part puzzle, part life. The labyrinth is art.

Life Without a Daybook

I am going to make time stand still.
This poem will not speak of excellence
but of beautiful emptiness, the thrill
of a long beach stretching beyond existence
into the morning sunlight and vanishing
where the mermaids sing.

If you are waiting for my return, don't
bother: my flight is one way and the urge
to get back doesn't appeal at all.
I've left behind a spread sheet that won't
spread, a computer crashed in a surge
and everyone I need to call.

I have left a message on my machine
suggesting you do the same and run
away. It isn't hard. Just let go. Green
and sensuous islands await you; sun
will caress you as half-naked you stand
on the edge of wonderland.

I can't tell you the time. My watch
got left behind, so don't worry about
having to be somewhere—you can catch
the sunset just by waiting. And out
there in the orange, aqua and turquoise
the splendor makes no noise.

Hammock

Yesterday, in the dead of winter, my shadow
greying with age upon the driving snow,
I wanted to stop the world and get off, slow
my heartbeat to a season's pace and go

quietly insane. But now, through fronds
spreading green fingers to part the night,
with my senses impaired by rum, I respond
to the hammock's sway and cup in my right

hand the moon which says *sing to me of
gentleness.* Orion's belt is worn by a temptress
begging me to rest in her arms. I confess
I know only happiness and love.

A thousand years ago an Arawak might
have lain here and watched the stars shine
like little fragments of tomorrow's light
offered in promise. And if his heart, like mine

wondered what would become of those
he loved and the places he knew, the ocean
replied endlessly with its rise and repose
and he got no answer but the motion

of drifting back and forth, leaving his mind
suspended in perfect darkness and uncertain.
So, who cares? The moon is being kind
to a stranger. Hello moon. Let's be lovers again.

Death Apples

*The leaves, bark and fruits of the Machineel tree contain
a caustic sap which may be injurious if touched. The trees
are common along Caribbean shores. Avoid contact with
any part of this tree.*
          —Roadside sign, St John, USVI

She talks to herself in dialect,
and if you listen she will mention
a son in New York, a daughter
in Miami, a brother driving cab
through a snowy Canadian storm.
Tides that surround this place
tell her of those scattered hearts,
the tug of what is left behind
balanced against a living wage.

If it rain today, the woman
says as she sits in the shade
of an almond-leafed tree,
*I think I suffer from all
the pain made of mankind,*
and crosses herself earnestly
and closes her brown eyes.
O my Madonna of the islands,
do not weep for us this way.

And when the rains come
in mid-afternoon, falling
in shattered silver tears
from a heaven that bleeds
for paradise, the market empties,
the tourists vanish, the buses
depart. Everything grows
in a riot of wild old green
and the earth stinks mightily.

When Columbus arrived here
he named the machineel fruit
death apples and slaughtered
the Arawaks who brought him
food for his hungry sailors.
For every paradise there is
a fall, a time when time
begins, a loss where sudden pain
rushes to fill the vacuum

as storm clouds fill an empty
sky. Thin white beaches braid
the inlets. Snorkelers stumble
in the current ripping reefs.
Tall ships sail by diffidently.
Come to the country of Eden
say the posters. *Taste the exotic.*
The woman beneath the tree
is selling a beautiful fruit.

Volcano

—near Soufrière

See how he comes from the blinding light,
the bright angel sounding his herald horn
and blowing time away, setting night

and darkness to their schools, ready to form
the new world. If you hear a story
it becomes your memory, for life is born

in the fire of minds, lives in the glory
of red-hot words, burns itself into
myth and story, cooling, leaving its hoary

pattern of Jack Frost tracery in new
layers of shape and meaning. This volcano
may explode but not before it is inside you.

* * *

Although it tries to be blue and different,
this planet is a child of the fiery sun,
screams like a child, boils like its parent,

sheds its veneer to show how it began,
stinks like something old and new
and seethes; and not to be out-done

by tectonic origins, the earth can do
terrible things with its calm, masked face,
hiding secrets in shades of green and blue

and spinning blithely through space.
Such is the Earth's truth and all things
share it, speaking for life and giving it voice.

* * *

How old is the Volcano? The question rings
in myth and science and there is no
answer. On the crater floor, sulfur stings

the rocks, rising from the stink holes aglow
with the puce jewels of perpetuity.
The way to measure time is patience, slow

surety, eternity borne with dignity,
an old woman walking a palmed avenue
and bearing a basket on her head. See

how each footstep moves forward, view
how her neck stands taut and her dress,
worn at the flowing edges of her life, imbue

a sense of solidity once painted by Renaissance
masters; and so in this we witness history,
the measured consolation of life and progress.

Now look at the bubbling mud and see
in its heat, steam and mineralized gases
another face: the sun's visage of eternity.

* * *

Once upon a time, a long time as time passes,
there was master and slave and sugar estates
where the forebears of this island bore lashes

for their labours and suffering for their fates.
And now, here, they watch the days go by,
wearing masks of smiles to hide their states.

I wonder what God made slavers, why
my ancestor, John Newton, should think a hymn
would pardon boatloads of suffering, why

any grace, amazing as it may have been,
would excuse a soul from eternal punishment.
Hell is more than justice and less than whim.

The bowges and the rings were not heaven sent
but fanciful visions of poetic inspiration.
The greater understanding of suffering has bent

the minds of moderns away from divination,
and we look for lions on the written page:
the real ones are between us and our destination.

* * *

A band of Creole musicians on the stage
scratch out a soft, melodic and melancholy
waltz, a tune learned long ago on a strange

night, far out at sea, between Africa and unholy
shores; and through a drum made of goat
and bamboo, its skin chained and wholly

beaten into voice, the music speaks without
the manners of the great house but with the pride
which overcame the lash. This is not about

song but longing, not about return inside
another ship to a long lost world, but the strong
unspoken rhythm of old stories, set aside

by time but containing new truths, long
stories about how the world was made,
remade and made again in a reborn song.

And there is one tale of a man who made
an angel of himself, alive in the living flesh,
by falling in the crater's pot. The narrative said

he survived, plucked from the raw, fresh
blossom of inner earth, the mouth of Hell.
His name was Gabriel; and where the press

of all the fiery force of time rises, Gabriel
has left his name. The volcano is Gabriel's well.
We speak to the sun through the stories we tell.

Flamboyant Tree

—for Kerry

So what is the name of the tree? I ask.
Flamboyant. And for a moment, lost in speech,

we are silent. Comprehension is a painful task
when word and meaning lie beyond reach.

Because the eye is enamoured with exotic
colours, stunning whites, crimsons and pastels

shining like distant stars in the neurotic
progression of rich tropical green, my mind dwells

on the nameless tree, mistaking adjective
for noun, soaking in the unfamiliar tones

and learning a new word. What definition can I give
to this moment? You say *flamboyant.* One's

senses stall. The heat of a Caribbean day
stuns the synapses. Yes. It is *flamboyant.*

But the name remains a mystery. You say
it again and again, and somewhere distant

in my thoughts, like a recurring dream far, far
away in a timeless, fecund land, I recall

the first frost, the sudden shout of life for
one dying moment. I picture a red maple.

I know this. Don't tell me. Let me guess.
So, it's a flamboyant tree? You answer *yes.*

Orpheus and Eurydice

—for Dana Gioia

The incline jagged beneath his feet
and strewn with life's broken promises,
he thought she stumbled as she went.
A gentleman, he turned. The Shades
reached out and seized her. No! *she cried*
and slowly faded back among the dead.

* * *

The wasp nest in their first apartment
drove them from the Junction to the East
where they found a good place for rent
they could afford, and this, at least,
was closer to work. Not much above
the mean, but even so they had love.

Dancing on Saturday nights at the Rex,
she in her black tights, he in leather
fitted like a glove, they would fix
their hearts, minds and dreams on whether
they could make rent with just enough
to hang out on Queen and pay for stuff.

Tell me everything about yourself, he said
one night as they lay together, a train
through Monarch Park rattling their bed,
she with royal moonlight dying to drain
the colour from her pale breasts, a bird
tattooed on her shoulder, rising above the word

DENIAL. *Everything is impossible,* she replied,
when you can't say anything and turned away.
He stared at the ceiling snowscape. If she died
today or tomorrow, what would be left to say
about her, ten or twenty years from now,
cut off from her breath, her touch, the slow

rise and fall of her ribcage as she slept.
In the loneliness that became the moment,
the dark pit of silence between them, he wept
the tears that test devotion and spent
hours imaging where she had been,
what lovers she had had, reinventing each unseen

face, each touch, each erotic gesture
that meant a world of meaning to those
she no longer loved. And when the torture
became too much, he got up, put on his clothes
and walked toward the night. By the time he got
to Broadview and turned around, he forgot

the depths of his doubt; the daylight had
returned. The subway was running. He took
the train back East. She would be mad
when she woke and found him gone, look
for him in the street beneath their window
and invent her own unseen faces, shadow

and image and story to make it more real
and punish him with silence, perhaps flirtation,
more likely diminished indifference, to conceal
the feelings she could not share. In the station
as she boarded a car for work downtown,
he saw her, her back turned, moving on.

* * *

He sat by the river, lamenting her name,
letting every note he ever sang float
away as the sun-coined current came
to listen to his grief. And when he sang about
her to the stars, he prayed they'd hear his pleas
and having hearts, have hearts to break or ease.

Anna Jameson at Niagara: The Whirlpool

—for Molly Peacock

That morning in February when my ink froze
nearly broke my heart, the letter to Ottolie
chilled to the bone, the frail blue characters
chattering like teeth. Now, all that matters
are the words, the ones reaching from soliloquy
into conversations, drawing to a sudden close

the long winter and making springtime come,
a voice assuring the heart where a sojourner
faces the open road. This is a strange country,
full of possibilities, dreams undreamed, some
virtues, little pride and less passion. I harbour
resentment against lethargy yet love to see

the lazy giants of the forest slowly waking,
the leaf appearing from its sleep, my soul
reborn. In the dead of winter, the world
seemed a nightmare, the lake ice breaking
and rising in a wall of cheerless grey, the full
blanket of death white and deadening curled

around the house with all the stilled malice
of a deaf parliament. Here, I could easily
have gone mad if not for the imagination,
the tiny pearl of April hidden in a secret place
where dead world's fingers cannot pry, delicately
warm and still alive, the anticipated consummation

of soul and intellect made daft by dull Toronto.
And when I first glimpsed Niagara, buried
beneath the veil of its own breath and heavy
with the ice-bound pain of its own grey flow,
my heart sank, my expectations dashed. I hurried
into despondency and forgot the wondrous cry

that echoes *Nature! Nature!* within my soul.
And yet a little life remains. Of that I am capable.
And I sat upon Table Rock and watched the surge
pulse and course and press beneath the ice, unable
all the while to hear my heart's beaten song. The urge
to despair flooded my being. In that moment of dull

and vivid emptiness, I drowned in my own life.
But today, returning here with spring, in earshot
of the roaring waters and cradled like a babe by
sunlight and warm, free, open air I forgot
myself, forgot the winter and the reason why
I came to Canada, nobody's ornamental wife

for a few blissful hours, only my own self,
my own new world waiting to be discovered
and claimed, body and soul, in my own name.
And this Nature is no man's world. I came
to realize it is woman's also. I have recovered
a land of my own devising, a place by myself

in myself and like a conquistador slowly
possess it. It is a hard quest, full of doubt
and mystification, the journey that so many
before me have denied themselves; and if any
have dared go there, the husbands shout,
the lords who think they rule and lordly

hold it over womankind deny us. We too
are sojourners. We too can make our way
in the world. Soldiers of the heart, making a land
from the clay of our desires, building a new
world from the stuff only slaves command.
This country is a work of the imagination, the play

of intellect flowing like the whirlpool below,
spinning and turning round and round and round
until we are free. This land was made by God
but it will be shaped by women. The slow
march of the seasons will not trouble us, the sound
of rumoured failure will not dissuade. The flood

is a thirst that cannot be quenched. And here
in earshot of Niagara, on the edge of an empire,
on the tip of a spring day's tongue, sits a word
as yet unspoken, and when it is finally heard,
when it is trumpeted and whispered, there
will be my heart's awakening, its life, its fire.

Billy Bishop

—for Barry Callaghan

A snowy field disappears in the distance,
searching for a hero it never knew;
and in the grey sky of unknown promise
a glint of silver starlight might scintillate
the silent dawn and offer to yet renew
the hearts of boys inside the men late
for work who wish they could chance
redemption and be, just once more, new.

This is a land of heavenseekers, of eyes
turned upward awaiting a return, of
Bill Barilkos disappearing in open skies
where their names are carved on grails,
and silent dawns rise wearily above
the flat roofs of Tim Hortons. The travails
of the heart are written in snow, the wise
travel their usual roads and deny love.

But just once, just once says the heart
as it beats out its steady and unflattered song,
I would like to face the dawn without
routine, without obligation, knowing each
battle is but a challenge of an old long-
forgotten ache, the pain that tries to teach
the man what he forsook for endless doubt.
Give me wings and wind, not right and wrong.

The airport is crowded with commuters,
with men such as the one inside this poem,
grey-haired, grey-suited, all rightly proper.
Beyond the security gate, the departure
lounge and the safety instructions, as home
disappears beneath us and the engines roar,
there is the open sky, the chill morning air.
That shadow on the fields is our own.

Angels

—*for Sydney Lea*

Brown summer lumbered along behind
neighbour men who sang to lawnmowers,
who stood at windows as August showers
hailed their hopeful gardens stained

with failed intentions. And I thought:
there is beauty everywhere; the sky falling
on power lines; the light after rain brought
a shimmering to the driveways calling

out like miracles in the desert. Having
wandered forty years in such joyous voids
and watched as the promised lands of loving
and certainty faded like old polaroids

of Ramblers in the labyrinthine frieze,
sad eyes still watch. And heaven sees.

Mr. Lill's

Pink pates shone as if aureoled,
reflecting the Saturday morning sun
that hung heavy with opinions
on the cigar-stale breath of old

men in Fred Lill's joint on Yonge.
Four generations beneath his shears
had risen cropped and prickly
from his chair. *Hold your tongue*

and sit still, he'd glare and threaten,
saying he kept tin ears downstairs
for unco-operative rascals like me.
The paper collar would tighten

to a choke, the striped white chasuble
was strewn with lost strands while boys
wild and golden-locked sneered
through the windows at the disciple

of the past who played an old man's part.
Smooth as a kitten's wrist and ready
for the Lord's Day to come, I was
Samson without Delilah and stood apart.

Antique Shop

—for Robert Sward

The pages of an old book open
to the smell of time, of words cast
on deaf ears or a jar emptied then
abandoned, filled with the last
hopes of redundant promises.
A portrait stares in silence.
At any price, the face vanishes
into a future it could not face

like Nosferatu afraid of the light.
When people gather these pieces
together and call them precious, might
they be clinging to the faint devices
of real hope? A silver bowl tarnishes
beneath a parasol. A sleigh rides
the wall uphill. In the past's silences
the present's mirrored face resides.

Do you ever wonder what people
see in the past, how in brown
corners life once rooted supple
fingers and tried to hold on—
how like the joints in a chair frame
the linkings failed, loosening
and growing apart until only name
held the pieces to their belonging.

Step cautiously in front of a looking glass,
tinted, originally, to hide blemish,
to absorb the truth. Let the image pass.
These are not sad things. They embellish
life but do not live. They speak of us
in silly ways like footprints left behind
on a beach where the sea has vanished,
and the tide line is drawn to assure the land
of what cannot be vanquished.

The Shadow

The story of this house is one of shadows;
of those who shaved in front of their shadows,

who painted shadows and hung them on walls,
who built the house simply to see the walls

and see beyond them; for every shadow
is part of a family, a shadow of other shadows,

an echo of light even through darkness,
a spark which says *I am alive* and darkness

which answers *you are not.* I dance
with my shadow because the dance

is a way of betraying the language
which the shadow cannot speak, a language

only a shadow can understand, a verity
falling amid conversation, a verity

ending a conversation. The shadow is a poem
waiting to be read, or the silence after a poem

is finished and its world is made of a shadow
standing in the beauty of its own shadow.

The Learning Process

—for Carolyn

A favorite dress could harbour death.
Playing music crashed the Market.
Joy dared not draw a muffled breath
in this strange dance of cause and effect.

* * *

My sister and I grew up listening
to poems and grammar over dinners,
every swallowed phrase digesting
deep inside us: we fattened on primers.

Our father at the table with a book
read of Blake and innocence as night,
peering in the kitchen window, looked
on in uncomprehending darkness, the light

too brilliant to bend or break or fade.
In our family it took four generations
to honour happiness, to be unafraid
of joy, to shed our disconsolations

where wonder hung its head in fear
and music cleft the heart in two;
with studied courage we took each year
as a reward and made another day new.

And so, from this plain faith we profess,
our family story moves slowly along.
Love's long shadows stand by us
as angels round the cradle in a song.

Appling

Even the air tasted of apples, clear,
sweet, ripening our cheeks to red
and turning the ash and birch to gold.
Braced between a V in the hold
of an Empire's arms, or spread
atop a Macintosh with no fear

of how far to fall, my reach
would often exceed my grasp,
sending a Newton lesson clattering
down on my sister's head to teach
her how things fall, then clasp
an unsteady branch without shattering

next year's nodes and descend.
My newly widowed Grandmother
loved a good basket of Courtlands,
sauced or baked, could pretend
to all that sadness was some other
person's, that her twig-like hands

held up to gather down the haul
shook with surprise and not grief
at the ripening of the bountiful year.
The moment punctuated by windfall,
a sudden momentary burst of belief
in something everlasting, drew near

and slipped away, the one beauty
we couldn't reach, so red and ripe
and just too high. Courtlands are hard
apples, but they keep well, doing duty
long past the season snows wipe
away, leaving only shadows in the orchard.

Mavety Street

—for Kerry

When moonlight stole like guilty cats
            and summer owned the air
I kissed your lips on Mavety Street
            and tousled your starlit hair.

Grave windows on the darkened rows,
            the abandoned dairy's shell
cast off their grimy prose of life
            and wished two lovers well.

The old men in the Balkan Hall
            looked up from losing hands—
my love I pledged on Mavety Street,
            more heart than head or glands.

Your tiny flat was heaven's realm,
            the roof leaked sylvan streams,
but you and me together there
            was daylight to my dreams.

And moonlight stole the years away
            and summers drank the air,
I thirst for that kiss on Mavety Street
            and the starlight in your hair.

Rugged

—for the grandchildren of W.W. Dennis

Sun glinting off the lakes below,
a land like a mirror someone broke,
pierced through the Jenny's wires.
When he landed, he always spoke

of wind, the way an updraft rose
like a revelation over new territory,
the way the world receded timidly
like a shy animal, staring, slowly

backing away from offered pemmican
and gradually being coaxed back
less afraid of human hands and clothes
smelling of soot and engine smoke.

Lying beneath the stars at night,
counting the constellations as friends,
he reinvented the war, the Junkers
closing on his turret, the ends

of his twin cannon shooting stars
that fell into Germany, fading
in the echoing announcement
of peace, as he dreamed of trading

the breathless air above Frankfurt
for the silence of a northern night.
When it came to pass, lying there
in the cold and prospecting the bite

of frost that tasted as clear as water,
he listened, drew in a deep breath
and thought he could contain the vastness.
On the rainy Toronto day of his death

he found the level horizon, the edge
of the world just there beyond the prop,
and needful of the perfect lake for landing,
rolled to the north and flew on non-stop.

Speaking Chinese

1) Ernest Ludwig Meyer, 1865-1953

A Chinese dollar coin with dragon,
rampant, contains an ounce of pure,
high-grade Mexican silver. In years
of trouble it was a shelter for worth,
spoke of stability in interesting times,
elegance in the face of worthlessness,
the stuff of countless myths and legends.
I found one in my father's coin box,
a token passed from hand to hand,
the badge of lucky money, put aside
for a rainy day, glinting of sunlight.
As I sat in Mr. Lill's chair, the shop
would rumble and shake. Lill rested
his cut-throat and scissors and looked
disparagingly at the wall that stood
between his barber shop and Sam Lo's
Laundry next door. "That Meyer Brother's
machine will shake us to smithereens."
And later with my hair shorn short,
my father took me into the darkness
heavy with mystery and steam, the scent
of lye and bleach and cloth-crisp heat,
past an old woman in a blue silk coat,
to the inner sanctum of the back room.
A dragon snarled from a red calendar.
Red, the colour of money. White sheets
rumpled in a ball reposed like sad ghosts
on a mending table. White, the colour
of death and the light through a window,
curtained. An ancient man, his beard
thin and pointed with strands of fine
white silk, his head covered in a skull cap
and a pigtail left over from Boxer days,
nodded gently from a shadowed corner.
A younger man, a man my father's age,

entered through a door of clattering beads
that chattered like a skeleton suddenly alive.
He smiled at my father and greeted him
in Chinese. "Your grandfather," said Sam,
"was a very clever man. He'd come and talk.
Talk and talk. Could out-talk us at our own
tongue." The old man nodded and broke into
a language that sounded like a bird twittering
to the dawn. "He says he'll teach you how to
talk, make you like your granddad. Talk Chinese.
Ho sang yi. Good business. *Tung sui.* Bluing."
The chlorine smell of *lin fwum* stung my eyes.
A steam press hissed and belched like a dragon
as the old woman folded two ghostly arms
in a gesture of serene eternal rest. The story,
I was later told, was that *gui jin* Meyer,
a boy from Missouri, made his way on foot
to Canada with the patent for an early washing
machine and became a wealthy industrialist;
went bankrupt in the Crash of '29,
and undaunted, taught himself Chinese,
traded goods for cash and Chinese cash,
and gradually rebuilt the family business
in bluing and buttons and collar starch,
haggling in tongue with Chinese launders
and out-talking them in kind. As an old man,
who'd seen his fortunes rise and fall and rise
again, he dressed each morning in a clean shirt,
buttoned his waistcoat and white kid spats
and carried a Chinese dollar, just in case—
with dragon rampant, its tongues spread wide,
resplendent in silver and armoured in claw,
the fire in its belly stoked for the fight.

2) Ida Evelyn Reid Miller, 1893-1975

They spread the dragon cloth before her,
reciting her name in a litany of love,
"Miss Reid, Miss Reid," they said through tears,
as they poured her tea and wished her luck.

Marriage, they said, would be a journey,
and far from the girls of her Sunday class,
she would be alone, like Christ, in a place
without water, in a place without charity.
The green cloth would serve her well.
A dragon, embroidered on soft green silk,
danced in a field of finely stitched flowers,
a land not unlike that lot to the north
where she and her bridegroom would build
their house, the meadows before them alive
with colour, a delicate tracery of the divine.
She lowered her eyes and saw her image
floating among the jasmine flowers,
and thought of times her girls had cried
when families left Canada and returned home;
times when the patriarchs in smoky rooms
had pointed their fingers to the horizon
and thought of all they had left behind,
the broken country, the language they spoke,
the ribbon of iron, the landscape they broke,
men whose hands were gnarled by rock
and ties that bound them in silent tongues
to a place beyond gold mountain's vista.
"Now you must travel to barren lands,
where the desert is cold and fields are empty
and the only drink to ease a thirst
is the faith you carry, as Jesus taught us,
Our Father, who art in Heaven...thy kingdom...
Ky-tow. When you bow your heads and speak
your hearts, you are lifted up, you are one
with God." Teach us, they prayed, that we
may walk, on crooked feet our fathers bound,
through frail lives our skin has made,
in forests and words and seas of pain,
that we may be blessed and forgiven our trespasses,
as we forgive those that trespassed against us.
They smiled through tears and daintily bowed.
Be true to us. Remember us. You are our teacher.
And as she lay dying in Wellesley Hospital,
her brain and language wracked by life,
she repeated a phrase in unknown words.

A young RN named Gladys Chong
phoned one night from the graveyard shift.
"Your grandmother," she said softly so few
would hear, "is telling us to bow our heads.
Ky-tow. She asks that all the children pray."

Elegy for a Grandfather

I used to smell it on his hands—
the sour scent of marigold blood,
the green dying and undying spring
that sang to the sun of love.

It is springtime once again.

And when he bent to ease a stalk
and the sad heads struggled high
after rain had poured out life,
turning them in dismay to tears

(it is springtime once again),

he would say there's no end to it,
the planting, the weeding, the light
making small miracles happen,
bright colours run together

making springtime once again.

His hand held tight the soil,
his grip and strength passed to me,
my hands browned by too many hopes
yet digging in the past for more,

my garden, a blank page, is spring,

and that moment long, long after
the sun has set and the plants
grow accustomed to their fates—
the thin frail fingers in the earth

that first cold night of wondering...

Though it is spring once again,
I will not let this endless dying
wither his work, the scent of love
and quiet supplication to fate,

and that springtime, forever once, again.

Garden

—for my Mother and Father

To be a gardener is to question, anticipate
success where none should be, and pray
to a presence no one has seen. Love and hate

enter in the equation, the way a weed
infiltrates a patch of columbine; violets
surreptitiously invade lilies. You need

to have the will of a caudillo, the secret
megalomania of a politician, the pure seeing
of a *cognoscente*. A garden is a place to forget

the body, to touch without need of being
touched, the song at the centre of the soul
which says to all things living and growing

let me guide you. The world began for all
in a garden. This is where life gave birth.
You touch God when you touch the earth.

* * *

Why was it that Paradise was a garden?
Surely a mountain is closer to the divine;
the sea is full of life and it is known

that air is essential to existence. Define
any beginning and the same pattern of
flower and path, bed and planting combine

to form one picture: a garden is love.
One summer, while staying just outside
Canterbury in England, I dreamt of

Paradise, of a place so fine my guide,
Saint Augustine, wept as he did that day
of his conversion. And I wept too, cried

for a place I had lost, for a time and way
protected from the world; and awoke
remembering that Paradise, so far away,

was my childhood garden. The Ancients spoke
of Eden and separation in the same breath,
watched life run its course beneath a yoke

of suffering and courageous desire. Death
was also a garden. Ecclesiastes says we bear
the seasons knowingly and in that breadth

of stoic understanding, saw the clear
image of a flower tended by invisible hands.
Each summer the work and pain, the near

exhaustion and sweat for growth demands
patience, the sufferance of a bedside vigil,
watching a fine life slip like measured sand

through the dry throat of time, yet shored
by the love that person gave whose eyes implored
us to carry on because we were adored.

* * *

A flower is both vehicle and tenor, the head
emerging from the soil to first make sure,
then the test, the promise, the long limbs fed,

feeding on air, form one idea: to endure.
When drought came, it sought certainty in deep
roots like questions into the past; and more

sun brought new expectations, vows to keep
with time, strange treaties forming fast
alliances in chlorophyll and cell; then the leap

of faith, the moment when all desires of the past
announced themselves like the climax of love,
a shout in the first dawn of a June day, a blast

sounding the silver note of purpose to prove
but one thing—a flower. And so, the cosmos
blooms. A constellation of stars forms a roof,

the leaves a horizon; for everything grows
stronger with each moment a summer gives;
and a seed is a house where the universe lives.

Cancer

You could comfort me by speaking
of presence rather than absence,
of days made from just living,
of his smile, his walk, the dance

he would do to amuse a child,
the pose he would strike in comic
gesture. Not the dying, not the wild
stampede of pain, the deep oceanic

darkness he must have known
as he sat looking from the upstairs
window on the greying winter snow.
And by turning away from layers

upon layers of difficult images,
each wrapped in the memory of
suffering, we lose the life. Pages
of black, unwritten lines. Love

without anyone to take it. Crying
without tears or grief that goes on
deep inside ten, twenty years of lying
and indifference later. What was done

cannot be undone, and slowly
the name of our plague is said.
Break it to him gently—
it is *cancer.* He will soon be dead...

I am going to be a father soon.
Life has a way of anticipating joy
and finding a way to it. A room
full of relatives will gather to toy

with the new face, comparing
that chin, those ears, the little eyes
to those who stare only from the glaring
prisons which adorn the walls...

Will I see you again, I wondered
on that last evening when good-bye
would have signaled defeat, the floundering
wreck of hope's last voyage. Try

to be brave, I thought. But death
is a shared experience. The dying
leave pieces of themselves behind, bereft
reminders of what and who dying

took—empty slippers, a drooping robe
on a bathroom door—and that presence
which was once so real, so full, hope
once tangible and permanent...Since

I am on the subject, the subject of cancer,
let me tell you that it eats faith.
It is a question without an answer,
the wind which steals breath

from the living, making clergy and philosophers
into stupid, meaningless, wordless
blunderers who cannot profess or proffer.
Anyone who has stood by, helpless,

comforting the dying through their pain
will tell you what cancer takes—
it devours our courage to be human,
just enough, so the heart breaks...

That chin, those ears, the little eyes,
sleeping in the arms of my beautiful wife:
renew me with life's wonderful disguise.
Make my living worth the price of life.

At T.S. Eliot's Columbarium, East Coker

—"In my beginning is my end; in my end is my beginning."

No mean little hole in the wall, but a place
fit for embarkation on a long cold journey
where the traveler returns with his face
altered by the highways and mountains
his soul has conquered, where the only trace
of the spirit is in the silence that strains
to rise above the weight of its own gravity.

Anything is capable of taking flight, even
the word for a niche where ashes are stored—
columbarium—speaks of wings spread and drawn,
beating thin air, a homing, a migration or return.
The lectern where the gospel nests, a golden
eagle in Victorian brass, cannot be ignored:
the verses hatch. What rhythms can we learn?

I was talking with the verger who pointed out
the granite plaque. His eyes were rheumily tired
like one who had cared too long and thought
too hard about the details of a little-visited
corner, a place tuck-pointed and neatly swept,
kept kempt for the faithful, the message revisited
like a text: *be patient until time has expired.*

If you are going to believe in anything, then
choose to believe in poetry, a dimension where
time never tread, an eternal still of summers when
a rose never lost its perfect bloom and beauty
and truth walked as naked and free of sin
as Adam and Eve. If it sounds promising, there
is still room to imagine paradise and eternity.

And here, in the mossy scent of last Easter
and the solemn white lilies that became poetry,
perhaps time does move a slow pace faster
and the dead see beyond the end of temporality
where the great everlasting poetic Master
rhymes death with breath and life with strife
knowing in the end of ends there is only life.

Four Lullabies for a Newborn Daughter

—for Katie Charlotte

1) The Presence

Not a shadow can be seen
in the silent February dawn;
the mute reference of green
lurking in the rhododendron,

the changes taking place inside
the world's passive sleep
brought winter to its knees. Beside
you, as you lie waking deep

in the warm covers of our bed,
I listen to a small voice
calling us from a time far ahead.
Do you hear it? The city noise

of a disgruntled morning cannot
awaken us as this, the promise
of a hand held out to us, fraught
with all the joy and wonder a wish

for life can contain. The presence
is here. We shall call it child
and name it for the April essence
of sunlight innocent and wild.

2) Where Did You Come From?

If I imagine palaces of gold
or exotic islands without suffering;
if I dream of ancient forests and old
hills like hands and eyes forming

in the tomorrows of the womb—
they could not chart the smile
you shine as your room
absorbs the morning light. I'll

lift you gently in my arms
and wonder at the miracle you are,
part daylight, part distant star,
a traveler home from the storms.

3) Baby Song

Softly now, the world must rest.
Let us put our language to the test

and dream and sigh and wish all well
and slumber the sea in a spiral shell.

Little one, more precious than love,
let me sing with you to the stars above

and slowly as the morning light appears
I will let your coos allay my fears.

The world beyond has much to say;
but we'll leave that for another day.

For beautiful are the simplest sounds
how intricately each breath resounds

as you whisper the miracle of your birth
like starlight dancing down to earth.

4) The Intercession

I will not let the stranger in the door;
the hour is late, my child is sleeping
and the shadows on the cold street pour
their grieving hearts out. I am keeping

watch over a promise my parents made
one night in the summer before my breath,
and with their sighs shield those afraid
of life from the reckless courage of death.

Chinatown

A summer rain falls and dampens the smell
of limp brown bok choy draped from boxes
collected on the curbside of Spadina Avenue
as an old woman turns over a ripe durian,
touching its spines with a scientific curiosity
and feeling its flesh for soft spots in the green.

A streetcar inches on as the light turns green
and from a dim sum doorway comes the smell
of onions wokked in sesame, a curiosity
for the nose to ponder like opening strange boxes
and discovering sensations, like tasting durian
for the first time and navigating Spadina Avenue.

This is an awakening. Here on Spadina Avenue,
the prose of North America and its Whitman green
is overlaid by the eastern wave, by lichee and durian
and air so ripe, so livid with the bright smell
of being somewhere else, that Euroness boxes
in around the Euroed soul and all is curiosity.

And the mind dances. It jumps with the curiosity
that tormented navigators who sought an avenue
to pepper trees of perfect gardens, Pandora's boxes
forcibly opened, gun boats and opium and green
horizons for the thirst. And beneath it all, the smell
of tainted history, a restlessness prickly as a durian,

smelling as putrid as the ripe and chosen durian
the old woman has dropped, catching the curiosity
of eyes distracted momentarily and the raw smell
of fullness and death echoing down the avenue.
O Paradise, once East of Eden, place of perfect green
and still as Li Po's moon, collected in Chinese boxes

and crated wholesale to the British Museum and other boxes
where ghosts sequester culture—like that ripe durian—
has become the stuff of truth, the simple joy of green
fruit professing the torment of mankind. Curiosity
bids one turn for a second look and the long avenue
of time, broad and crowded spreads ahead. The smell

of torment boxes us in, yet attracts us like a curiosity
in a trading company, like a durian broken on the avenue
and the soft green meat's timeless, inanimate smell.

The Correspondent

*But if man is to find his way once again in the nearness
of Being he must first learn to exist in the nameless.*

—Martin Heidigger, *Letter on Humanism*

1)

He returned to his beloved's country house,
a thatched cottage, picturesque, where ducks
paddled in a decorative pool. She bent
willow-like and scattered bread, her image
shimmered and he recalled the horizon.
For a moment, he could not speak her name,
though once in the desert he dreamed it.
He wanted to tell her what he'd become,
his heart a windstorm, his words sand.

Dear Stranger, he began his story, *I come
from a place that has not yet happened,
a dream in the mind of a dying man.
But how to begin it and how to end it.
Narrative is an hourglass full of sand.*

2)

Strangeness of the language was the first
shock to his system—his ear tuned to nouns

lost track of sentences and he wandered
among thoughts, an *ingenue* in the bazaar.

Here everything became a verb, objects
floated around his hotel room, fan blades

slowly buffeting them as they settled
beside him in the post-meridian scorch.

The light through slatted olive shutters
slipped like telegrams beneath the door;

NEWS FROM HOME; STOP; EVERYTHING; STOP.
Going up country to report a disturbance.

He dreamed rivers drier than Victorian prose,
and sands shifting to reveal lost names.

3)

The camels behaved badly at first, belched
and farted, making the air its own story,
where facts became suspicious and distorted.

Flies that buzzed secrets in his deafened ears
were like beggar children demanding coins.
His skin drank too much. The horizon danced

to the tune of harness bells and the heat
rolled off streams of columned linotype
for which he would offer himself as byline.

Sand jammed the carriage of his Underwood
and on a single sheet of clear white paper
he struck the word TREE in roman uncial.

As the sun roared over the immobile hours
he took refuge beneath that word and waited.

4)

Listen said the TREE, *you can do without
the porters and the baggage, the sage advice
of guides and maps and all the names
that will take you where you do not want.*

He put his hand over the page, gave the TREE
a shadow, palm fronds spread in the sun.
His editors were shocked at the colour
of his reports:

...everything here is black
and white. There is a prophet who camps
beneath an ancient tree while the heat
dances across the nameless desert. He says

men passed this way a week or more ago
and carried guns toward the border hills.
Stains of their shadows litter the sand.

5)

One part of his memoirs is most memorable:
a civilized man must bring nouns to a place
where only verbs exist. Life and death

are verbs, states of being, copula and personal,
possessive and prepossessed. The desert was
and is and ever shall BE swallowing objects,

hungry for adverbial rain, Ishmaeling adjectives.
His caravan came to an oasis. Children played
by the village well. Women dressed in black

stood patiently like furniture in storage.
What of the war? he asked through his guides.
No one seemed able to understand. They shot

his porters, trashed his typewriter. A problem
in translation or simply a local custom.

6)

When you do not wish to be misunderstood
you must always become yourself, and that
is like telling a good story properly—facts
can easily get out of hand, mere words
ring like churchbells to the pleasant
candour of their own sound; someone
always spots places where you go wrong
and the world is full of cowards who cannot
face the truth about themselves. In war,
you must lie according to your own
misconceptions and make them seductive.
If you cannot sound convincing, the facts
will always bear you out. Be inventive with truth.

—from A Handbook for Correspondents, p. 173.

7)

He rode south with the sun as his guide
and made good his escape before night fell.
He shivered beneath the stars and named them.

His reports recorded civil strife, bodies piled
between startled palms, and how, by night,
he had slipped away, his byline still intact.

We live in a troubled language, he mused,
where words overflow with implicit passion
and desire becomes the hemlock of truth.

He sat in a City pub, pouring gin over lips
healed from their scorching by simple facts,
remembered how men gave up their shadows
in life and death, verbs calling out for nouns,
palms raised to heaven pleading to be read.

8)

And years later, when they found his body
they said he was a brave man, an honest man,

a good man, a simple man. They said he was
a man of letters, a man who should not have

gone away, a man whose place became misplaced,
a man whose time had come too soon. Here

was an absence waiting to be missed. Funny thing,
death happens only to those in linear time,

in things named and claimed and places owned.
He owned nothing. It's like that Heidigger quote

at the beginning of the poem: he found the nameless.
He would have appreciated that. He loved stuff

that made sense in a different zone of logic.
He's there now, loving every minute of it.

9)

So, he began with a conclusion in mind
for that is the nature of all beginnings—
that at the root of every failure is a word,
and beneath that a voice, more distant
than a foreign land, whispering names
among the bones of Eden. Once, long ago,
one would have dreamed the impossible
and by pronouncing it become a prophet;
but the world became a catalogue of dreams,
and all one needed was a pair of eyes.
He looked at his hands. One spoke around
the truth, not through it, and he had come
to the other side, leaving behind a lifeline,
a telling trail in his own nameless dust.

Success

When I die I want to be remembered
as someone who succeeded in life;
and the more I try, the quicker I approach
that successful end. In triplicate, strife

bids me fill out its requisite forms, one
for accounting, one for the files
and the last for the system. When done,
only the firebreathing system smiles.

Please name an award for pointless
dedication after me and present it
to the next overachiever who climbs
the mountains of paperwork and shit

in the pursuit of excellence. A wall
is not an obstacle to a bricklayer.
A door is an opportunity, not an exit.
Remember the fool dragonslayer.

Ithaca

—for Alfred Corn

If I wasn't such a devoted husband
I'd be a terrible womanizer. Just
watching the waves, I come to distrust
my self-control. Life is to understand
oneself and grow old knowing I will hand
on the kingdom to a son barely old
enough to dream of paps. The death cold
sea threatens me with bony epithets, and
I have to admit that I am a coward
who does not believe in great adventures.
All the prow-eyed ships point toward
Troy and the waves are speaking censures
to those who would stay at home. I board
my fate, leaving all to chance and foreign shores.

And as the place called home grows small
and shrinks behind me like lost nights
of love and mixed emotions, the sun ignites
the fire in me and responsibility is all.
In my spare time, I picture that grove of tall
laurels beneath stars where we camped
and sang and got drunk and trampled
on people's crops in search of good game.
That was a country to believe in, a place
made fine because it made me, a name
cut into these lips with my first cry. I trace
its mountains in my sleep. I wake and tame
the wind with oar and sail. The commonplace
is what's heroic, but it will never be the same.

Still, you've got to weigh the benefits
of being a hero. After all, if the dice roll
in my favour, if I use my head, my goal
of becoming a bigshot could benefit
the kingdom. Penelope could buy clothes fit
for a queen. No more groveling over overpaid
servants. Send to Egypt for a decent maid.
I could get a new chariot. And the exits
of Hades are going to be clogged with fools
because these are foolish times and everyone
wants to get ahead. In a world of fools,
where do I fit in? I foresee blood, the sun
bleaching fine bones. We are set to schools
where the gods let few pass; and there is no lesson.

Except home. I truly believe there are some
things, gentle things that make the going
worth the trouble. I picture Penelope sewing
on the porch, the light of a rainy, lonesome
summer afternoon floating about, a handsome
son growing tall and strong, calling me Dad,
following me through the streets. If I had
been a great man, full of passion and regard
for pain and suffering, I might easily frown
upon someone like me—types who pull hard
on life's oars and stare the rough fates down
knowing we can't win but working toward
the project of our own dignity, happy to own
a little piece of the world, if only a backyard.

Jonathan's Porch

—for Jonathan Barron

It's the first time in ages I can breathe.
The azaleas are blossoming as if death
has been undone by the bright love

of a Mississippi spring as you give
me a cool drink and slowly I believe
in life again after a long leave

of absence from myself. I need
to feel the air in my lungs to prove
that I have not lost myself, have

not forgotten what poetry is and above
all, how to relax. The off rhymes weave
through our lives and yet we believe

in the beauty a child can achieve
as she draws a stick man and we feed
on the speculations of words and deed,

knowing the heavy summer rain will relieve
the stoicism of all the unachievable
dreams we imagine. It is good to breathe
again and the azaleas are happy to be alive.

In the Garden of the Istituto

—for Antonio D'Alfonso

Far from the Villa Medici, the Villa D'Este,
in the silvered light of a humid afternoon,
the keepers of culture have their way.

This party is a vestige of the past, the day
of art and beauty having passed too soon,
far from the Villa Medici, the Villa D'Este.

Ours is a strange paradise. An array
of lilacs bravely announce their bloom:
the keepers of culture have their way.

It is impossible to murder art, we say,
but our century has struck that tune
far from the Villa Medici, the Villa D'Este

and its discordant melody fades away
like embers; but whatever the fire may consume
the keepers of culture have their way—

for the light is only slightly tarnished today
and over glasses of wine their whispered orison
far from the Villa Medici, the Villa D'Este:
the keepers of culture will have their way.

New Year's Day, 2000

Today I look from my window
on the flowering of a new millennium.
The old century has stolen away
taking with it the waning darkness,

the faces of the time that shaped us
and the history which shamed us
into love. Some said this would be
difficult, that the world revolved

around time. But this morning
there is only grey-blanketed snow,
the footsteps of our child awakened,
the warmth of your hand and the future.

What cannot be forgotten shall be
guidance. What cannot be understood
shall remain. I am not without hope:
the wind lies cautiously still.

Bruce Meyer was born in Toronto in 1957 and holds a B.A. and M.A. from the University of Toronto and a Ph.D. from McMaster. He has taught at various institutions including Trinity College in the University of Toronto, McMaster University, the University of Windsor and Skidmore College. Author of fourteen books including the poetry collections *The Open Room* and *Radio Silence*, the baseball short stories *Goodbye Mr. Spalding* and the textbook *The Stories: Contemporary Short Fiction of the English Language*, he is Founder and Director of the Creative Writing and Professional Writing Studies program at the University of Toronto School of Continuing Studies. He lives in Toronto.

"It is difficult to describe the central virtue of Bruce Meyer's fine new collection because its particular quality is so rare in contemporary poetry. Despite the admirable diversity of the poems in *The Presence*, which range from lullaby to elegy, from reportage to myth, the book is unified by a kind of impassioned equipoise, a dynamic balance between contrary forces—emotion and intellect, hope and fear, imagination and the senses—in which both impulses are recognized without either being granted the upper hand. *The Presence* is Meyer's most arresting and accomplished volume."

—Dana Gioia

"To discover Bruce Meyer is to discover a voice far more Frostian than any to Canada's immediate south. Like the master, Meyer is uncannily canny with form; yet like him too, he offers speech so convincing and credible that it gives the lie to the tired claim of free verse propagandists; that meter and rhyme inhibit 'natural' diction. *The Presence* shows a wonderful author in full command of his more than considerable endowments."

—Sydney Lea